WILD ABOUT ANIMALS

CROCODILES

By Martha London

Kaleidoscope
Minneapolis, MN

The Quest for Discovery Never Ends

······································

This edition first published in 2020 by Kaleidoscope Publishing, Inc.

No part of this publication may be reproduced in whole or in part without written permission of the publisher.

For information regarding permission, write to
Kaleidoscope Publishing, Inc.
6012 Blue Circle Drive
Minnetonka, MN 55343

Library of Congress Control Number
2019938720

ISBN
978-1-64519-001-1 (library bound)
978-1-64494-243-7 (paperback)
978-1-64519-101-8 (ebook)

Text copyright © 2020 by Kaleidoscope Publishing, Inc. All-Star Sports, Bigfoot Books, and associated logos are trademarks and/or registered trademarks of Kaleidoscope Publishing, Inc.

Printed in the United States of America.

Bigfoot lurks within one of the images in this book. It's up to you to find him!

TABLE OF
CONTENTS

Chapter 1: Silent Predator **4**

Chapter 2: Hidden Beneath the Surface **10**

Chapter 3: Life in the Water **16**

Chapter 4: Protecting Crocodiles **22**

- Beyond the Book 28
- Research Ninja 29
- Further Resources 30
- Glossary 31
- Index 32
- Photo Credits 32
- About the Author 32

CHAPTER 1

Silent Predator

A large **Nile** crocodile suns himself by a river. It is August in Kenya. Food is on its way. He can feel the **vibrations** of thousands of hooves. A huge **herd** of wildebeests is nearby. Every year they cross this river. They are searching for more grass to eat. That is good news for the crocodile. He could use a big meal. All he has to do is wait.

Crocodiles live and hunt near the river.

The water is fast and deep. It is no problem for the crocodile. He has a strong tail. It lets him swim through the rushing water. The wildebeests come down the riverbank. They know there is danger in the water. But they need to eat. Grass is on the other side.

Hundreds of wildebeests run into the water. They want to get across quickly. The crocodile slides into the river. He watches the splashing animals. There are young wildebeests in the herd. They are not as strong as the adults. One struggles in the fast water. The crocodile sees her. He sinks under the water.

He is a large crocodile. He could take an adult. But that is more work. The young wildebeest is still fighting to get to shore. She is tired. Other wildebeests are passing her. The crocodile begins swimming toward her. She doesn't see him in the cloudy water.

FUN FACT
Wildebeests travel over 600 miles (1,000 km) on their migration.

Millions of wildebeests migrate every year to find food.

7

He is next to the wildebeest. The crocodile leaps out of the water. His strong jaws clamp down on her leg. He is much heavier than she is. The crocodile drags her down. He rolls his body under the water. The wildebeest drowns in the river.

FUN FACT
Crocodiles swallow stones to help digest their food.

The crocodile takes his meal to shallow water. He rips off pieces of meat. He swallows them whole. This was a big meal. He won't have to eat again for weeks.

Crocodiles hunt wildebeests in the water.

CHAPTER 2

Hidden Beneath the Surface

A saltwater crocodile floats in the river. She stays near the sandy shore. Her eyes and **nostrils** are on top of her head. Her head is triangle-shaped. Only her eyes and nose are above water. The rest of her long body is hidden.

The crocodile is covered in scales. They are hard. Her scales act like armor. They are colored light brown and black. She looks spotted. Under the water, she almost disappears. She blends into the river's sand and rocks. She doesn't see any **prey** on the shore. Maybe there will be something upstream.

Crocodiles hide under the water to wait for prey.

FUN FACT
Crocodiles have a second, clear "eyelid" to help them see underwater.

PARTS OF A
CROCODILE

powerful tail

eyes with night vision

pointed snout

armor-like scales

strong jaws

12

The crocodile moves against the **current**. Her legs tuck against her stomach. She can swim quickly.

She's an old crocodile. She's over 12 feet (4 m) long. This crocodile has been hunting this Australian river for over fifty years. All she has to do now is wait.

Crocodiles are good swimmers.

She is a patient hunter. She can hold her breath for over an hour. The crocodile knows something will come to the river soon. She waits. The sun shines down on the river. The crocodile finds a shady spot to hide. She doesn't want her prey to see her.

FUN FACT
Saltwater crocodiles are the largest living crocodiles.

Soon, a water buffalo comes to the water. It's a big one. But if she can catch it, the crocodile won't have to eat for at least a week. The water buffalo walks into the water. It's hot out. Everyone wants to cool off. The crocodile waits until the water buffalo takes a drink. Then, she lunges. She goes for the water buffalo's nose. Her teeth snap shut. But the water buffalo is too fast. It runs out of the water. The crocodile will need to find a different meal.

A saltwater crocodile's skin color helps it blend into its surroundings.

CHAPTER 3

Life in the Water

Crocodiles spend most of their lives in the water. Some crocodiles like rivers. Others live near the ocean. They hunt for food in the water. Crocodiles are **carnivores**. They only eat meat. Crocodiles surprise their prey. They wait near shore. They attack when an animal gets too close.

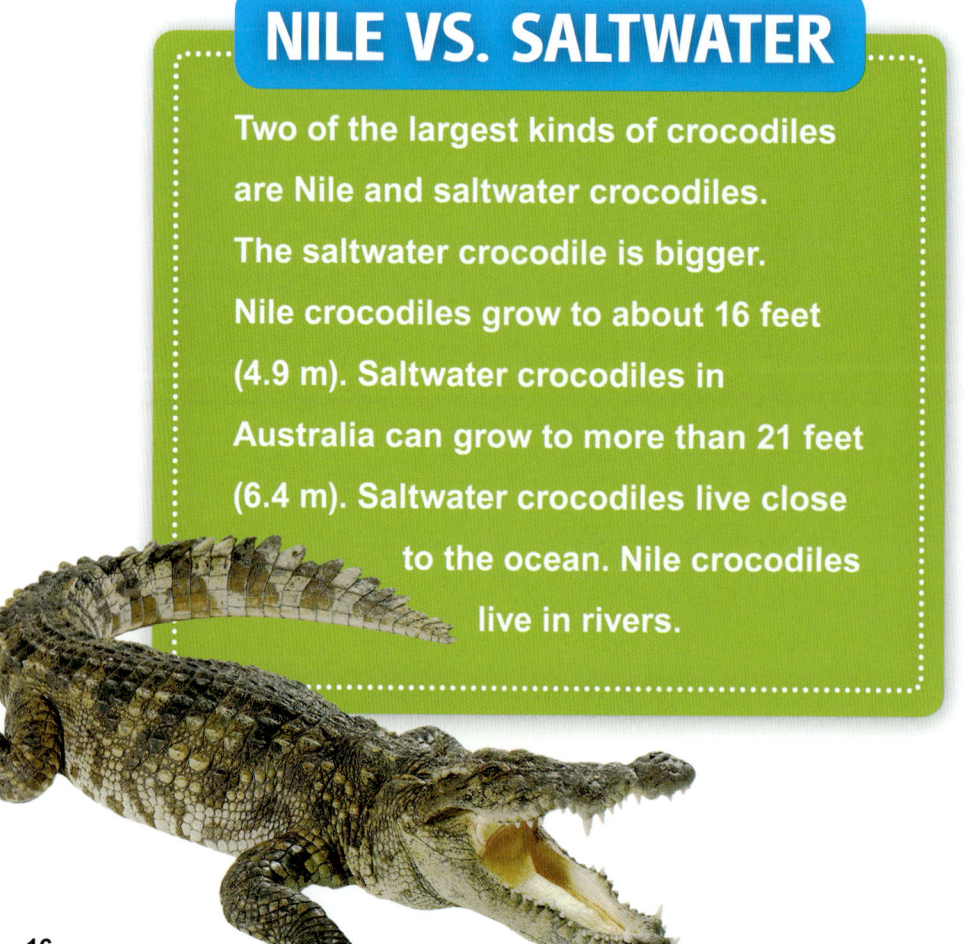

NILE VS. SALTWATER

Two of the largest kinds of crocodiles are Nile and saltwater crocodiles. The saltwater crocodile is bigger. Nile crocodiles grow to about 16 feet (4.9 m). Saltwater crocodiles in Australia can grow to more than 21 feet (6.4 m). Saltwater crocodiles live close to the ocean. Nile crocodiles live in rivers.

Crocodiles can live in rivers or oceans.

17

Crocodiles drag animals into the water. They are slow on land. But they are great swimmers. Crocodiles can swim much faster than most animals.

Most crocodiles hunt at night. It is easier to sneak up on prey. Their dark skin blends into the surroundings. Animals can't see them in the shadows.

Crocodiles lay in the sun to warm up.

When the crocodile gets cold, he has to get out of the water. Crocodiles are **ectothermic**. He needs the sun to warm up. The crocodile lays on the shore. The sun shines down. His body heats up.

FUN FACT
Mummified crocodiles have been found in Egyptian tombs.

Where Do Crocodiles Live?

When the crocodile gets warm, he might go back in the water. Or he might open his mouth. The crocodile's open mouth lets out extra heat. Crocodiles can't sweat. They need to find other ways to cool down. Some find a shady spot. The dirt is cool against their bellies.

Crocodiles need warm environments. They live in Australia, southern Asia, Africa, and Central America. The sun shines a lot in these places. It's perfect for crocodiles.

Most reptiles aren't social. But crocodiles are. Crocodiles play with each other. Older crocodiles give younger ones rides on their backs. Mother crocodiles are also good parents. They protect their young.

Crocodiles are social creatures.

CHAPTER 4

Protecting Crocodiles

Saltwater crocodiles and Nile crocodiles are not **endangered**. But African dwarf and American crocodiles are vulnerable. Vulnerable means almost endangered. Other species are critically endangered. They are Cuban, Philippine, Orinoco, and Siamese crocodiles. Laws protect them.

There are threats to crocodiles. People kill crocodiles and sell their skin. Crocodile habitats are threatened, too. A habitat is where an animal lives. Crocodiles lose their homes when people build new houses. This makes it harder for crocodiles to live. They need a lot of space.

People use crocodile skins for purses and belts.

People have started taking over crocodiles' habitats.

23

Most crocodiles are not dangerous to humans. But they are large. Many can be aggressive. People kill crocodiles because they are afraid. They trap crocodiles in nets. Crocodiles struggle in the nets. People use guns to shoot them. The loud bang echoes in the air. Then everything is quiet.

Saltwater crocodiles almost went **extinct** in the 1970s. Today, laws protect them. Scientists are also trying to teach people. It is possible to live with crocodiles safely.

16 feet (4.9 m)

HOW BIG ARE NILE CROCODILES?

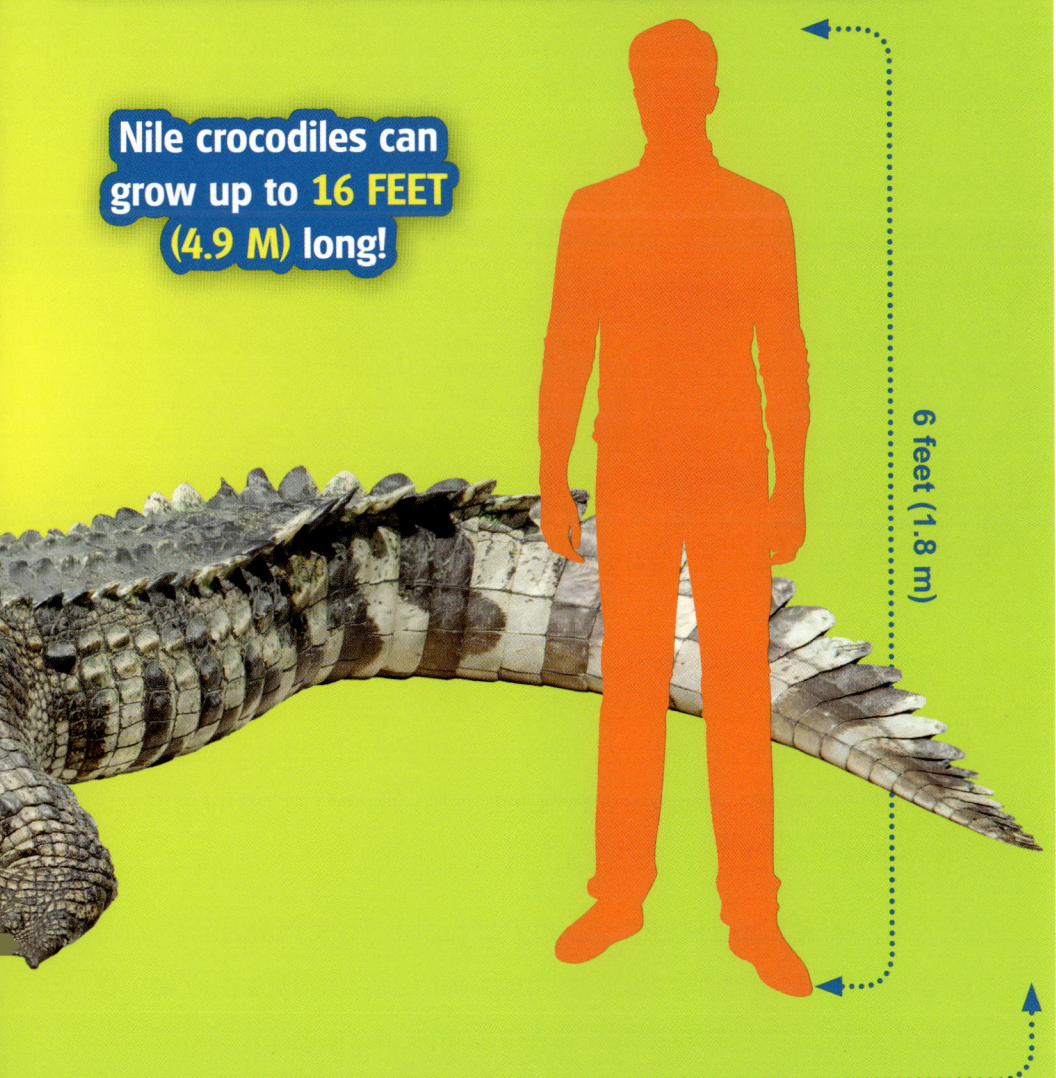

Nile crocodiles can grow up to **16 FEET (4.9 M)** long!

6 feet (1.8 m)

FUN FACT
Special crystals in crocodiles' eye sockets give them night vision.

Scientists try to learn more about crocodiles. But it is hard. Crocodiles are shy. They are great at hiding. Most crocodiles swim away from scientists. They do not want to be found.

Crocodiles also hunt mostly at night. This makes it even harder for scientists to find them. Scientists use large flashlights. The crocodiles' eyes shine in the bright light. Scientists count the number of eyes that they can see.

Crocodiles are important for ecosystems around the world.

This is a good way to guess how many crocodiles live there. But scientists must be quick. As soon as the light is on them, crocodiles duck under the water.

It's important to protect crocodiles. Even though people are afraid of them, crocodiles want to be left alone. Crocodiles live all over the world. They are very important to the **ecosystem**. They keep other animal populations down. Crocodiles help balance an ecosystem.

BEYOND
THE BOOK

After reading the book, it's time to think about what you learned. Try the following exercises to jumpstart your ideas.

THINK

DIFFERENT SOURCES. Think about what types of sources you could find on crocodiles. What could you find in an encyclopedia? What could you learn at a zoo? What about an interview with a scientist? How could each of the sources be useful in its own way?

CREATE

PRIMARY SOURCES. A primary source is an original document, photograph, or interview. Make a list of different primary sources you might be able to find about crocodiles. What new information might you learn from these sources?

SHARE

SUM IT UP. Write one paragraph summarizing the important points from this book. Make sure it's in your own words. Don't just copy what is in the text. Share the paragraph with a classmate. Does your classmate have any comments about the summary? Do they have additional questions about crocodiles?

GROW

DRAWING CONNECTIONS. Create a drawing that shows the connection between crocodiles and the health of an ecosystem. What would happen to the population if there were no more crocodiles? Think about how learning about a balanced ecosystem could help you better understand crocodiles.

RESEARCH NINJA

Visit **www.ninjaresearcher.com/0011** to learn how to take your research skills and book report writing to the next level!

RESEARCH

DIGITAL LITERACY TOOLS

SEARCH LIKE A PRO
Learn about how to use search engines to find useful websites.

FACT OR FAKE?
Discover how you can tell a trusted website from an untrustworthy resource.

TEXT DETECTIVE
Explore how to zero in on the information you need most.

SHOW YOUR WORK
Research responsibly—learn how to cite sources.

WRITE

GET TO THE POINT
Learn how to express your main ideas.

PLAN OF ATTACK
Learn prewriting exercises and create an outline.

DOWNLOADABLE REPORT FORMS

Further Resources

BOOKS

MacIntire, Francis. *Colossal Crocodiles*. Gareth Stevens, 2018.

Mattern, Joanne. *Alligators and Crocodiles*. Red Chair Press, 2017.

West, David. *Crocodiles and Other Reptiles*. Windmill Books, 2018.

WEBSITES

Factsurfer.com gives you a safe, fun way to find more information.

1. Go to www.factsurfer.com.
2. Enter "Crocodiles" into the search box and click 🔍.
3. Select your book cover to see a list of related websites.

Glossary

carnivores: Carnivores are animals that only eat meat. Crocodiles are carnivores.

current: A current is the flow of a river. The river's current swept away the young wildebeest.

ecosystem: An ecosystem is a location or place and all the living things in it. If one animal goes extinct, the whole ecosystem might suffer.

ectothermic: An animal that is ectothermic needs to heat up in the sun. Crocodiles are ectothermic.

endangered: A species is endangered when its population in the wild is very low. Some crocodiles are endangered.

extinct: A species is extinct when every animal of a species dies. Saltwater crocodiles almost became extinct.

herd: A herd is a group of animals with hooves. The herd of wildebeests crossed the river.

Nile: The Nile is Africa's largest river. The Nile flows through Kenya.

nostrils: Nostrils are openings in an animal's nose used to breathe and smell. Only the crocodile's nostrils and eyes were visible above the water.

prey: Prey is an animal that another animal eats. Young wildebeests are perfect prey for crocodiles.

vibrations: Vibrations are rumbling that can be felt. The crocodile felt vibrations from lots of wildebeests moving together.

Index

body heat, 4, 19–20

ecosystems, 27
endangered crocodiles, 22–24
eyes, 10, 11, 12, 26

hunting, 6–9, 13–15, 16–18, 26

jaws, 8, 12

laws, 22–24
living near people, 22–24, 27

nighttime, 18, 26–27

oceans, 16

prey, 10, 14–15, 16, 18

rivers, 4–9, 10–14, 16

scales, 10, 12, 22
scientists, 24–27
size, 13, 14, 16, 24–25
social groups, 21

tails, 5, 12
types of crocodiles, 4, 10, 16, 22

water buffaloes, 15
where crocodiles live, 4, 13, 16, 20
wildebeests, 4–9

PHOTO CREDITS

The images in this book are reproduced through the courtesy of: nattanan726/Shutterstock Images, front cover; Pimonpim w/Shutterstock Images, pp. 3, 12; PhotoSky/Shutterstock Images, p. 4; Ryan M. Bolton/Shutterstock Images, pp. 4–5; Jane Rix/Shutterstock Images, pp. 6–7; Sergey Uryadnikov/Shutterstock Images, pp. 8–9; EcoPrint/Shutterstock Images, pp. 10–11; Keith Michael Taylor/Shutterstock Images, p. 13; Meister Photos/Shutterstock Images, pp. 14–15; John Kasawa/Shutterstock Images, pp. 16, 22 (right); Janos Rautonen/Shutterstock Images, p. 17; Marina Demkina/Shutterstock Images, pp. 18–19; Red Line Editorial, p. 20; Steve Lovegrove/Shutterstock Images, p. 21; LuapVision/Shutterstock Images, p. 22 (left); boitano/Shutterstock Images, p. 23 (sign); Gianfranco Vivi/Shutterstock Images, p. 23; anek. soowannaphoom/Shutterstock Images, pp. 24–25; Chipmunk131/Shutterstock Images, p. 25; Stana/Shutterstock Images, p. 26 (eye); Rudchenko Liliia/Shutterstock Images, pp. 26–27; Pongsakorn Nualchavee/Shutterstock Images, p. 30.

ABOUT THE AUTHOR

Martha London lives and works near Saint Paul, Minnesota. She has written many books for young readers.